AMAZED

Aleksandra Artymowska

Laurence King Publishing

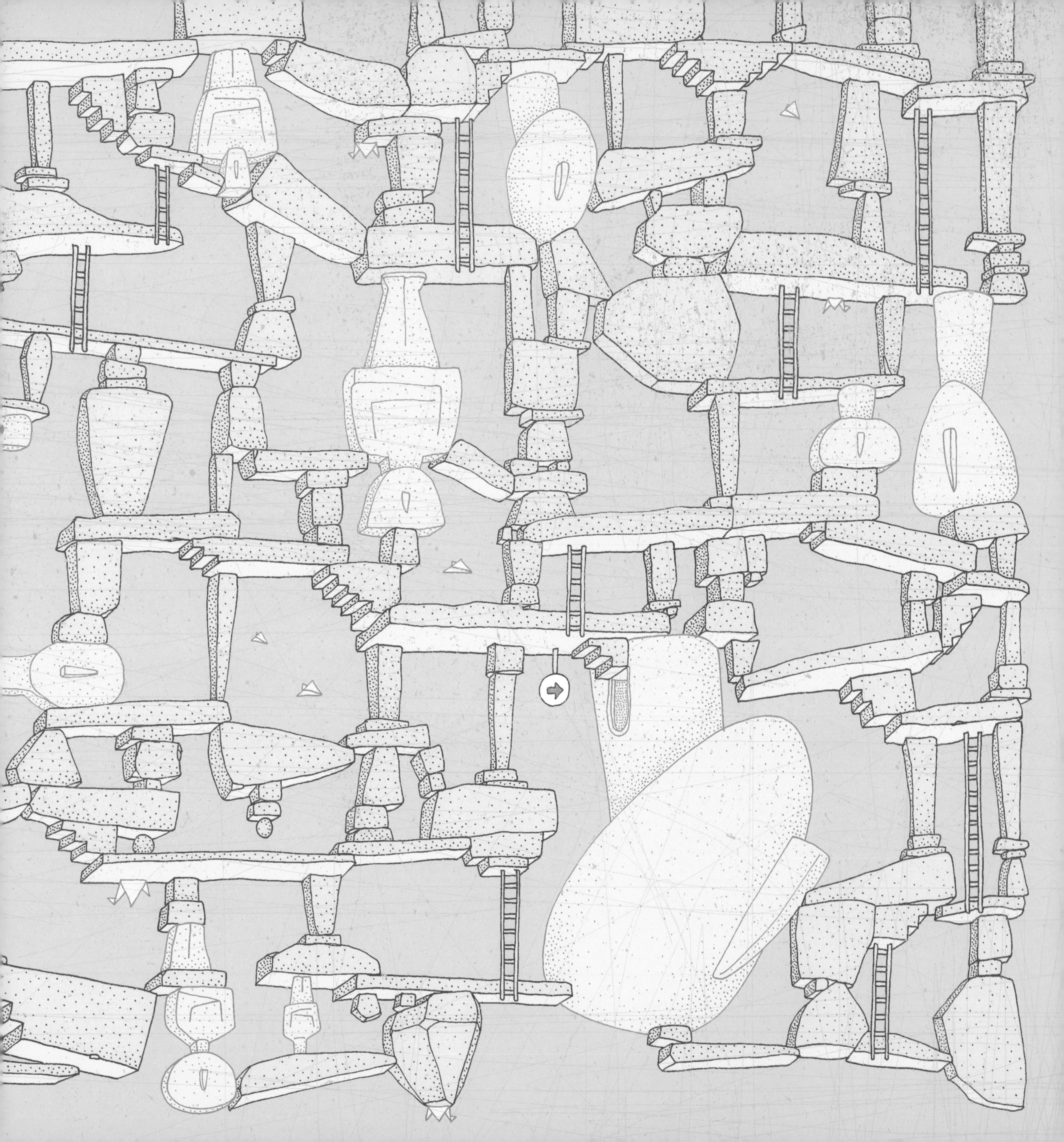

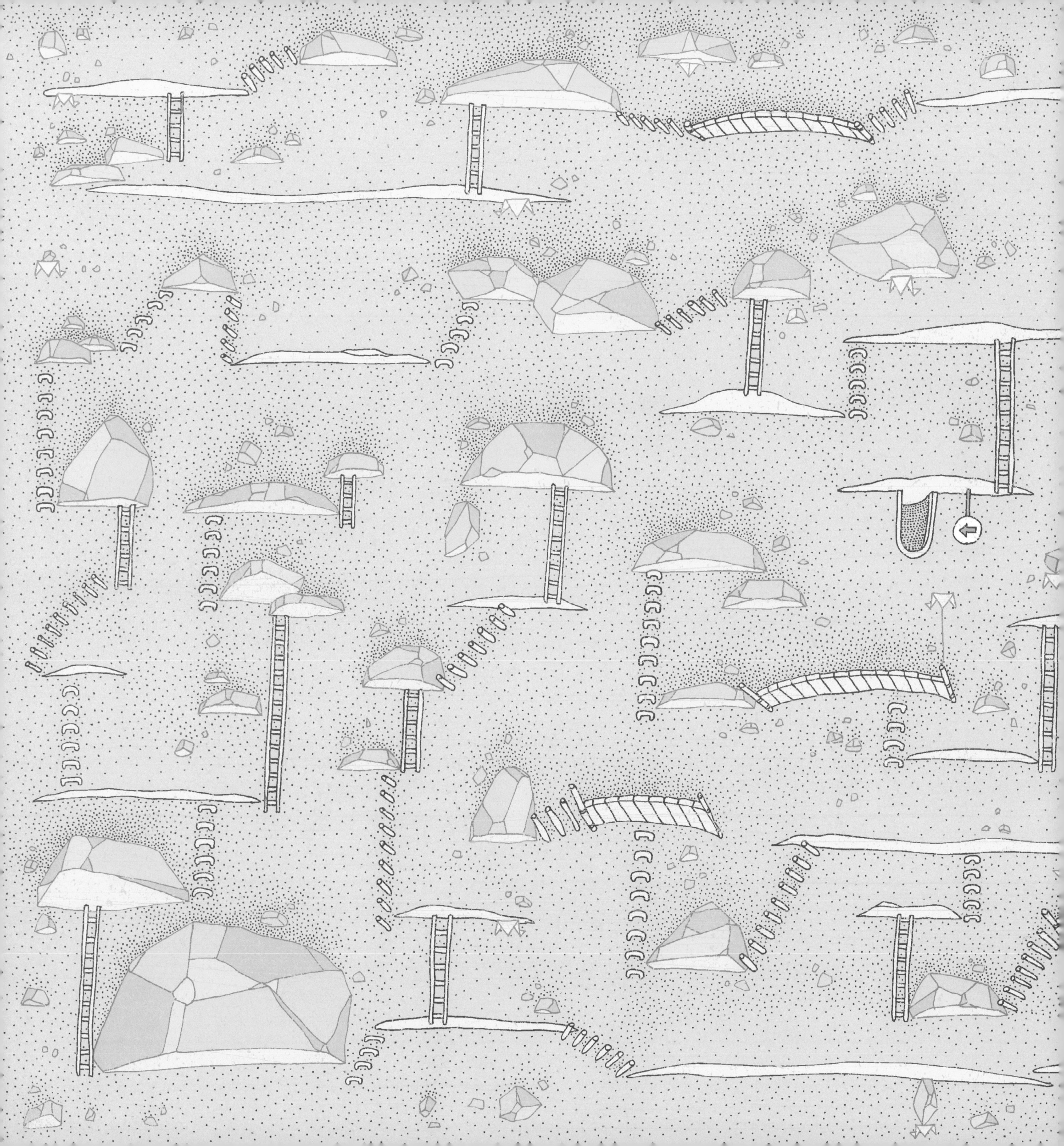

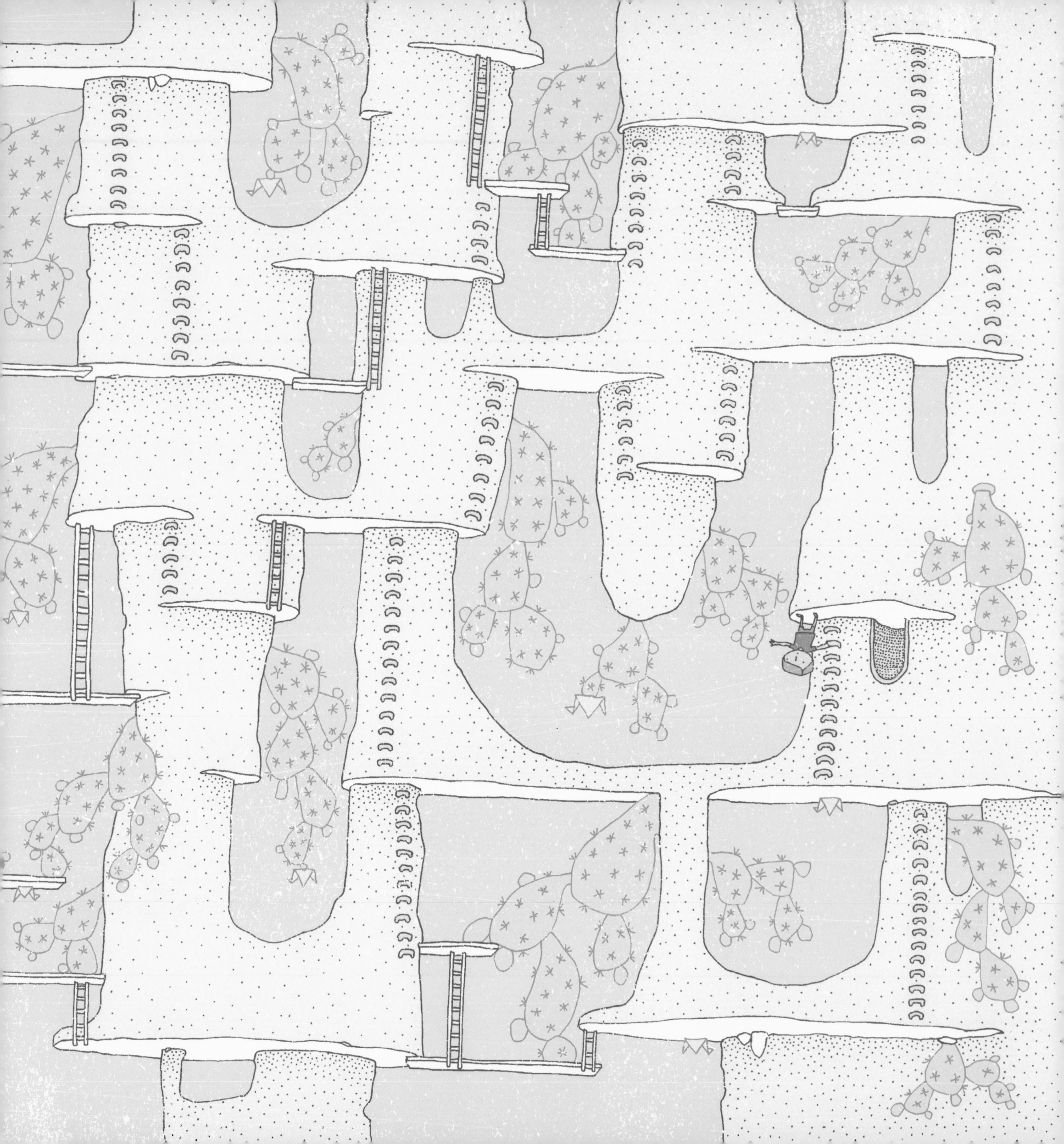

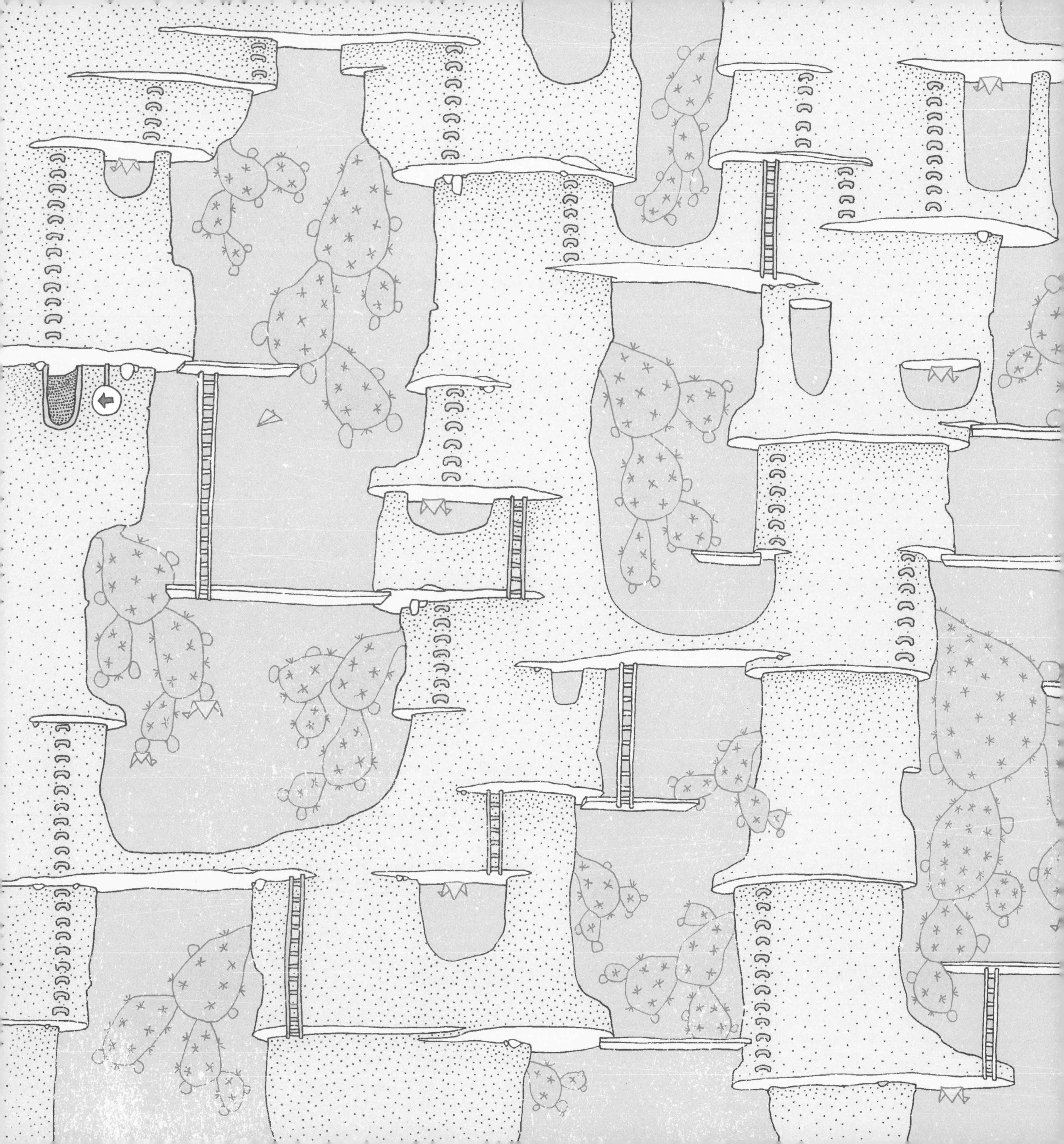

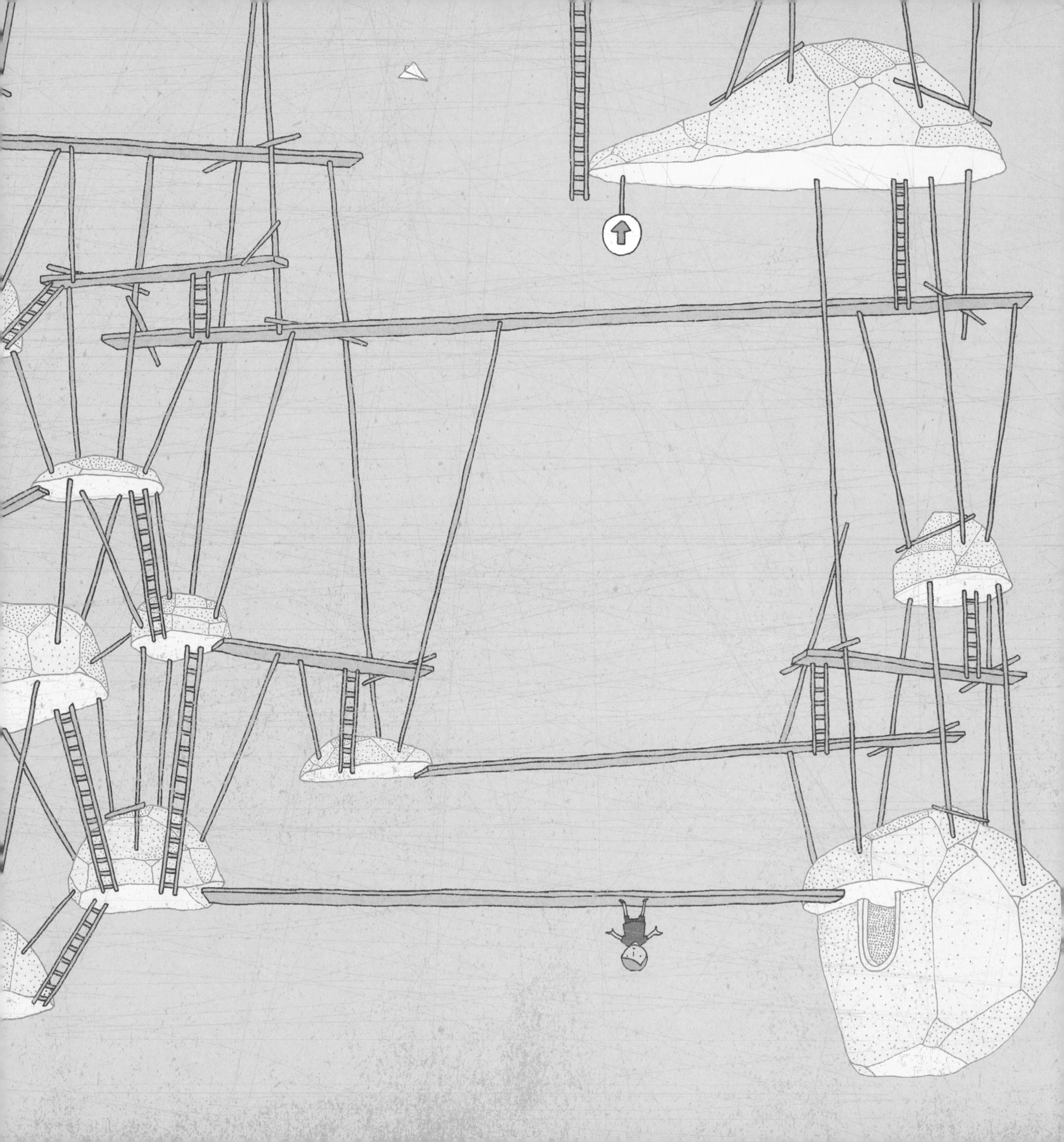

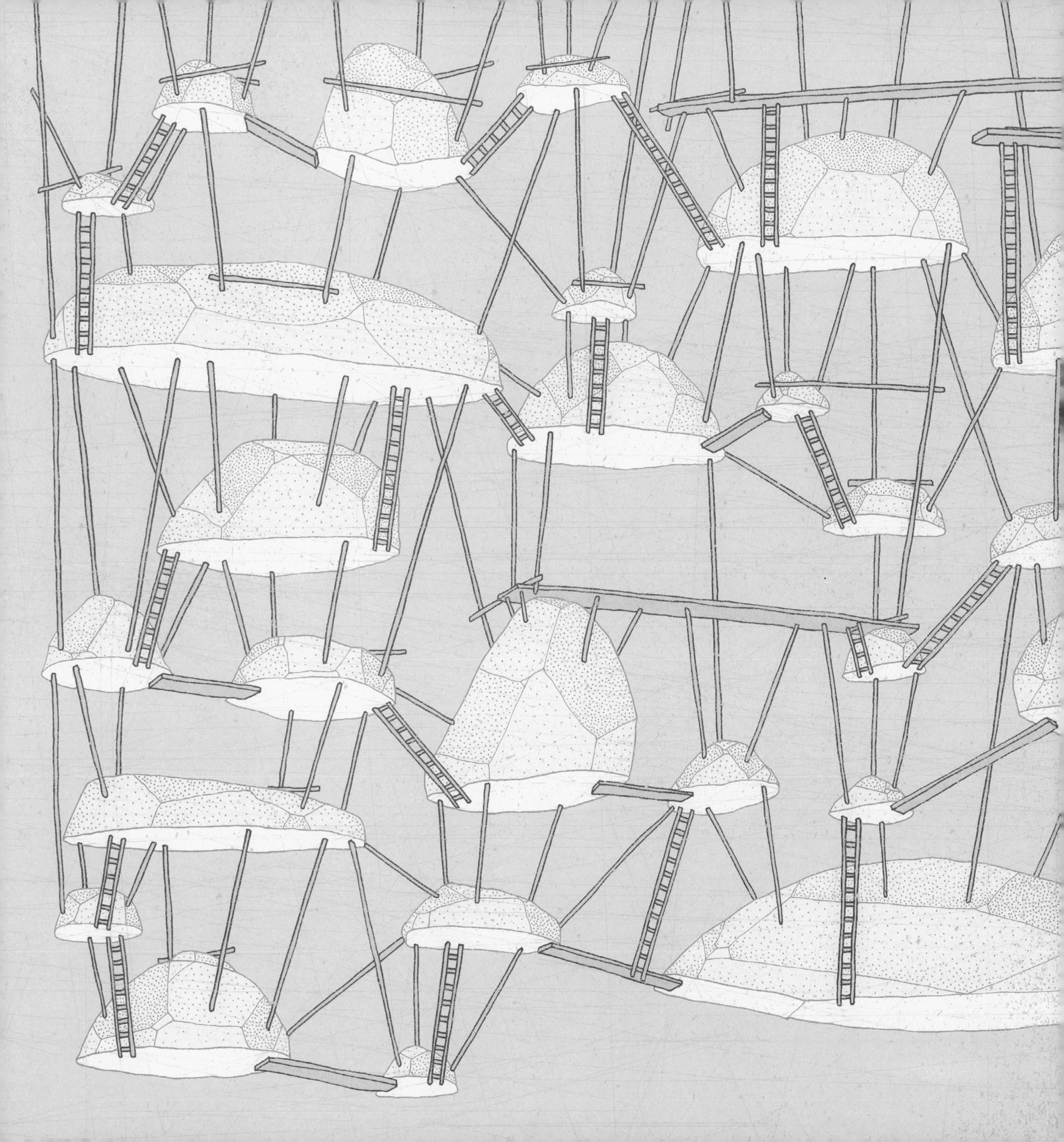

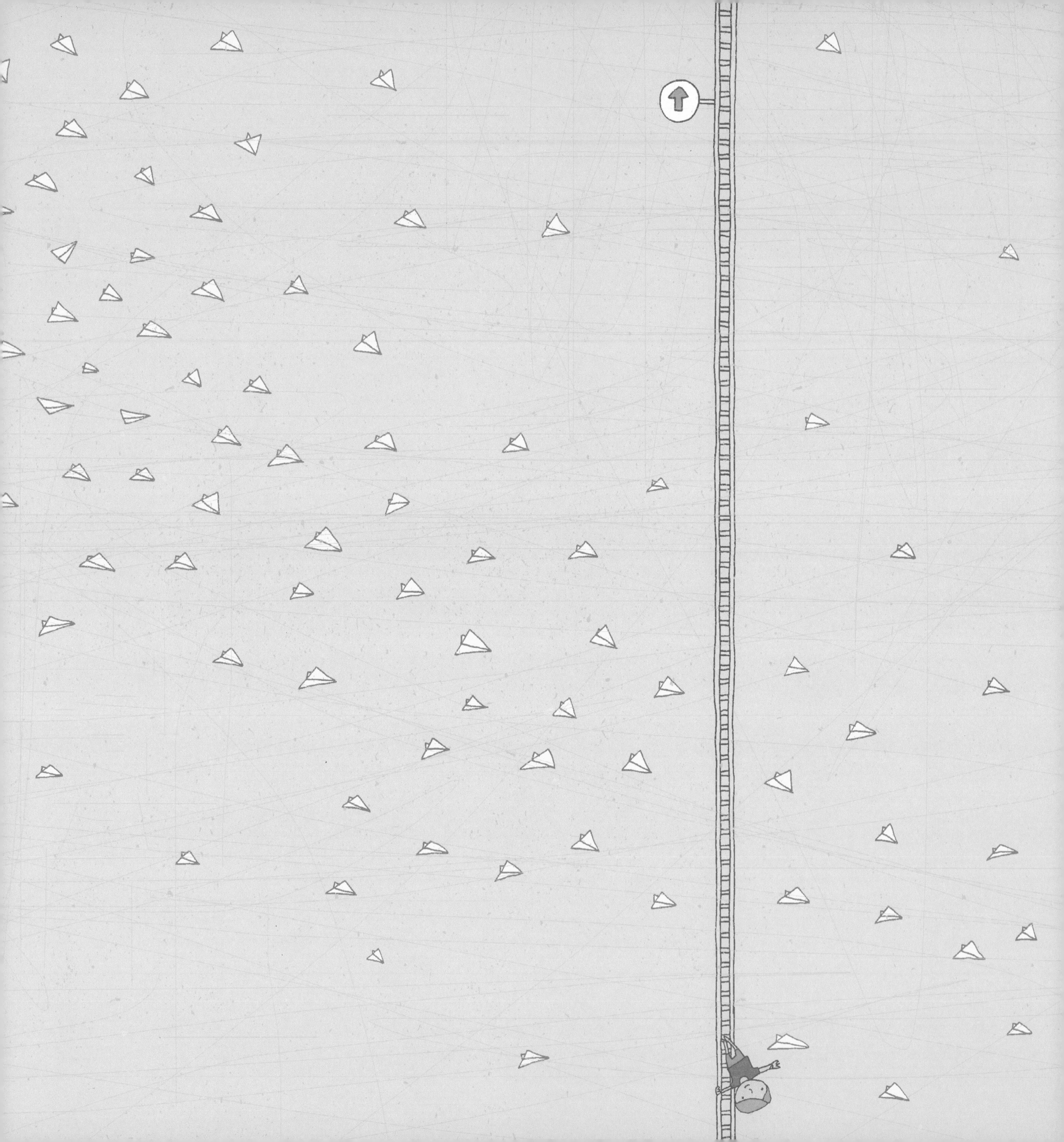

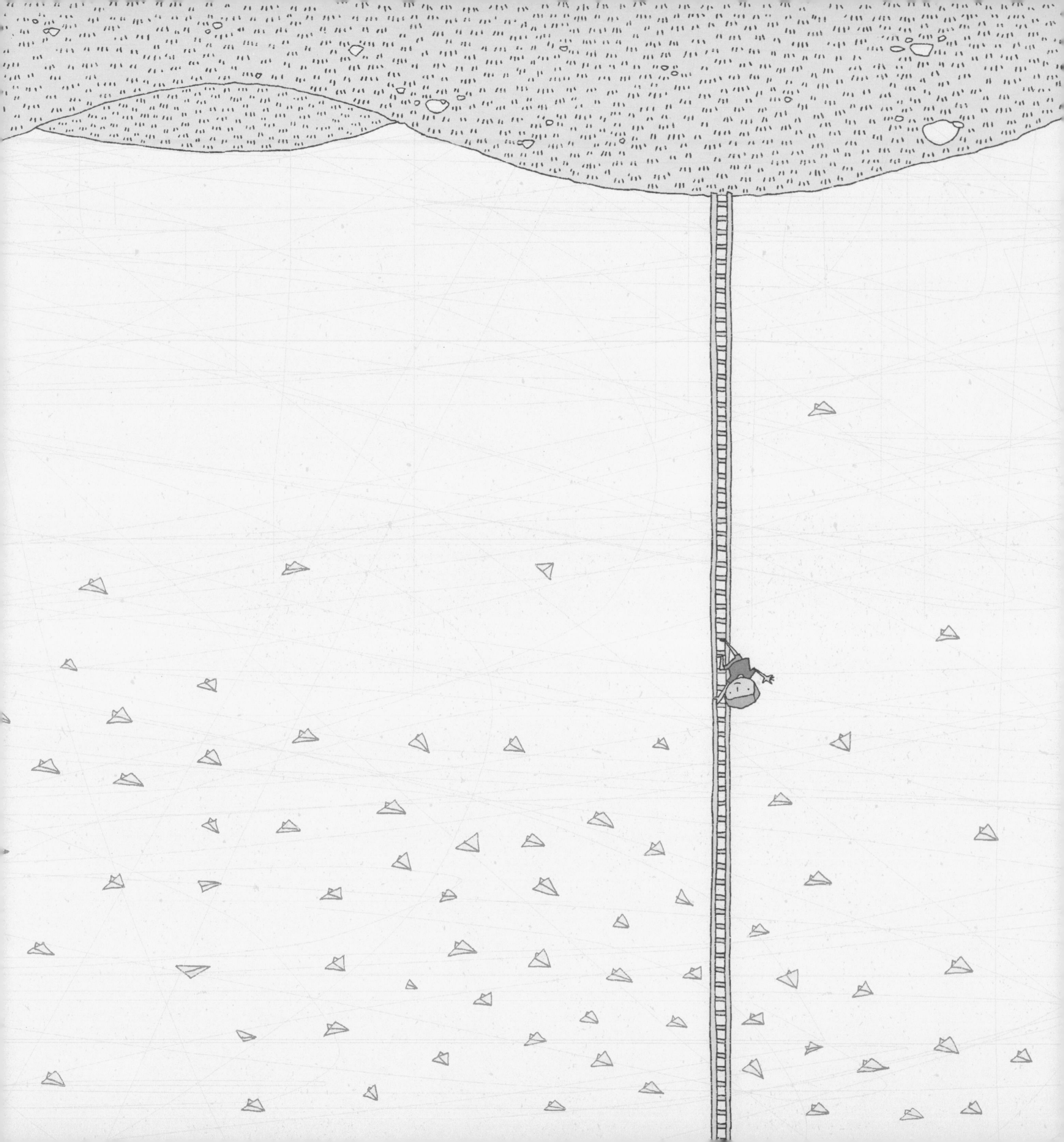